THE GRESH
A Lifetime in Show-biz

THE GRESH
A Lifetime in Show-biz

Carl Gresham

First published in the United Kingdom in 2009 by

Bank House Books

PO Box 3

NEW ROMNEY TN29 9WJ UK

www.bankhousebooks.com

© Carl Gresham, 2009

The Author hereby asserts his moral rights to be identified as the Author of the Work.

All rights reserved. No part of this publication may be reproduced, stored in a retrieval system, or transmitted, in any form or by any means, electronic, mechanical, photocopying, recording or otherwise, without the prior permission of the publisher and copyright holder.

British Library Cataloguing in Publication Data

A catalogue record for this book is available from the British Library

ISBN 9781904408581

Typesetting and origination by Bank House Books

Printed by Lightning Source

This book is dedicated to Helen, Steve, Sarah and Katie Farrimond, and to Jim and Sally Brennan.

Helen.

Contents

Foreword by 'Diddy' David Hamilton	ix
Preface by Derek A.J. Lister	xi
Acknowledgements	xiii
Introduction	xvii
People, Places, Events	1
Radio Days	57
Superslam Wrestling and the Foam Hands	63
Derek Franks	65
Finale	67

Foreword

I first met Carl Gresham in the mid-'60s. I was working as a television announcer for ABC TV, the station that provided weekend programmes in the North and Midlands. He introduced himself via a letter, which arrived at the Didsbury studios in Manchester. The letterhead included a huge photograph of him, so you knew right away with whom you were dealing. From that first letter I knew here was a man who liked to do it BIG.

In no time at all we were off on a whirlwind tour of the North of England. We must have appeared at every bingo hall, disco or supermarket that had an occasion it wanted to celebrate, coast to coast from Liverpool to Hull. Certainly we were the Kings of the Carnivals. One afternoon I opened three carnivals in three different counties before dashing to the TV studios for an evening shift.

I don't think there's ever been a company that had so many stars appearing in so many different venues on the same day, all arranged by the same agent. Each of us had our own card to hand out to any member of the public daft enough to want one. On one side would be our photograph with biographical details on the back. Somehow or other, no matter how big the star, Carl's name managed to appear more times than ours. These were 'Gresh' cards, and everything else was done 'Gresh-style'. Every year he sent me a card wishing me a 'Merry Greshmas'.

When ABC TV chose me to be Ken Dodd's 'straight man' in *Doddy's Music Box* in 1967 I soon earned the nickname 'Diddy David'. We broadened our horizons and went national.

We discovered we had three things in common: an enormous zest for work, having a laugh and earning money!

Once I was involved in a court case (a story to be told at another time) in Scarborough. By one of the great travesties of British justice I was forced to pay the costs. Not to worry. Carl fixed up a bingo appearance in York on the way home and the losses were recouped.

In 1971 I was booked to appear in my first pantomime in, of all places, Carl's hometown, Bradford. In fact, it was Carl who advised me what song I, as Buttons, should sing to the boys and girls in my 'Song Sheet' spot before the finale at the wonderful Alhambra Theatre. Should it be the classic and much-loved 'There's a worm at the bottom of the garden and its name is Wiggly Woo'? Not at all. Carl recommended I do the song from the British Rail TV commercial 'Travel Inter City like the boys do'. Such was my faith in the man I did it twice daily from Christmas until nearly Easter. I still have the publicity shots of me posing in my stationmaster's cap, waving a green flag. Was Carl getting free rail travel between Bradford and London? I certainly wasn't. To this day I still wake up in a cold sweat in the middle of the night, wondering how I became the first Buttons to sing the kids a TV commercial.

It was a girlfriend of mine who christened Carl 'Mr Cash Register Eyes'. She noticed that when money was mentioned his face went red, he rubbed his hands together and his eyes lit up like a cash register.

After me, Carl conducted whistle-stop tours with Bill Kenwright from *Coronation Street*, Frazer Hines from *Emmerdale Farm*, and Hughie Green – and I mean that most sincerely. And Carl is no mean performer in his own right. He has the radio shows and the pantos to prove it. Oh yes he has!

Who will ever forget his dear mother, who regarded us all as a bit of a nuisance, as we phoned Carl for more ideas of how we could expand our careers. I think she regarded show business with a healthy disdain, and wished her son had got a real job with none of these ne'er do wells. But Carl went from strength to strength, winning a contract with Woolworths – who booked over three hundred personal appearances by various stars throughout the country.

I can't think of any big stars Carl didn't work with. He knew them all, and because he handled all the personal appearances himself he knew them at very close range. With so many stories to tell it's high time he wrote the book. Let's face it, the man's a legend. And more than forty years after he sent me that letter with his photo on top I'm proud to call him my friend.

'Diddy' David Hamilton

Preface

I had a vision regarding the future popularity of Carl's book. I am walking in the valleys of Tibet, hungry, lost and in despair, looking for someone to point me in the direction of the capital, Lhasa. I pass an old man, and ask him, 'Which way to Lhasa?' He points me in the right direction, but before he moves on he asks, 'Where are you from?' I reply, 'Bradford, England.' He smiles and says, 'Do you know Carl Gresham?'

I have known Carl for some fifty years. His name was synonymous with the late 1950s when I, also as a young man, was starting up with my Rock and Roll group. The name Carl Gresham kept popping up in our world of Rock and Roll; as a DJ I was fortunate to meet many of the music stars of the day like Gene Vincent, Little Richard, Bo Diddley and Jerry Lee Lewis. Carl was and is a pushy individual (but not intrusive) where publicity is concerned, and he was always trying to get the celebrities onto programmes and shows he was currently working on.

The 'Gresh', as he likes to be called, has a marvellous memory which he can dip into for a wealth of stories about the film stars, people of the theatre and television he worked with when he was booking them for personal appearances through his agency. Most of them were, and many still are, personal friends. Here you can read witty, personal and poignant stories about Morecambe and Wise, Tony Curtis, Larry Grayson, Hughie Green, Pat Phoenix and the beautiful Jayne Mansfield, along with many more.

Carl's book has been a long time coming, and I know it will be a tremendous success, a book that should adorn the bookshelf of anyone who's interested in the world of show business.

Derek A.J. Lister

Acknowledgements

Helen Farrimond, for many years my partner. Helen had a remarkable attribute that many beautiful ladies have, and that's for knowing exactly what's right and wrong. She was able to stabilise my life and career and was always the perfect host. When celebrities such as Frazer Hines, Larry Grayson, Martin Shaw or Ronald Magill came to visit our house they all loved Helen and her hospitality.

I could never have wished for a better friend and confidant. When Helen later married Steve it was *Emmerdale*'s Frazer Hines who gave her away, as Helen's father had passed away some years before. I became Uncle Carl to their two girls Sarah and Katie.

Frazer Hines became a close friend, and remains so to this day. His continuous support and advice throughout my career has always been an inspiration, and to be in his company is always a pleasure. In recent years Frazer has lost a number of very close friends, and when Derek Franks died last year it made us both feel we need to live every day to the full.

Will Venters, producer of Yorkshire Television's regional news programme *Calendar*, has been a supporter of mine for many years. Thank you. He has always supported me, and encouraged me to get this book written and published.

Lesley and David Piper have always been encouraging me to write my biography. I know David from the pantomime merchandise business, and it was his lovely wife Lesley who did the portrait of me featured in this book.

Ken Rudkin was my business partner during the Cayton Bay days. We used to take it in turns to attend the events so we weren't duplicating our efforts and expenses! However, when it was my turn to host an evening with the beautiful

Alexandra Bastedo Ken decided he'd better come along as well; what a surprise. He has a terrific business mind that benefited both of us.

Ron Boyle was showbiz correspondent for the *Daily Express*. Sadly he is no longer with us. I was fortunate to accompany him when he invited me to see the great jazz pianist Oscar Peterson and singer Jonnie 'Cry' Ray. I was finally able to return the pleasure by inviting him to meet Alexandra Bastedo with me.

Derek A.J. Lister, my loyal friend and a major help in getting this book started. His guidance and experience have been invaluable, and I thank him for writing the preface to this book. I first met Derek when we were DJs in Bradford in the late '50s and early '60s, then didn't hear from him again for twenty years, when he contacted me about his book *Bradford's Own*. He wanted help tracking down various theatrical agents, which ultimately led to me being featured in his book. With three books to his name Derek's help and advice have proved invaluable. I hope I helped him when I organised a TV crew from our regional news programme to come and cover one of his many signing sessions in a local supermarket. For this particular one he had invited Bradford singer Kiki Dee. I only mention this because Derek hated me using my mobile phone while signing books. I did it for you, Derek!

Malcolm Porter has been a regular listener and guest on my BCB radio show many times. He hails from New Zealand and I love his accent. His travel stories have been marvellous and kept my listeners entertained for hours, along with his choice of music. He never misses my show, and for that and his friendship I thank him.

James Towler was a feature writer for *The Stage* newspaper and was part of the management team at Pennine Radio in Bradford. He employed me to do my *Relax and Remember* show on a Sunday evening. James sadly died many years ago, but I will never forget his kindness and support.

Peter Holdsworth, showbiz writer for the *Bradford Telegraph & Argus*. It was Peter who wrote about my stand-in role for Tom Courtenay in *Billy Liar*. So I got fired, but what can you do? I reminded Peter some years later, but he said it obviously hadn't harmed my career.

Jim Brennan and Bob Preston. Good friends who I must say a particular thank you to, for the time they helped me move my vast collection of records from one house to another. Over 40,000 singles and LPs to a second-floor flat! It's at times like those that you get to know exactly who your friends are. They remain close friends to this day. I would also like to mention Jim's mother Sally, who was close to my mother and another loyal supporter of my endeavours.

I would also like to thank all my colleagues at BCB radio in Bradford: **Mary Dowson, Jonathan Pinfold, Steve White, Ronnie Thompson, Janice Weale** and **John Pell**.

(above) Carl with his mum and dad.

(left) At the seafront with Mum.

Introduction

I started my career as a broadcaster, but soon ventured into employment as a columnist, disc jockey, actor, presenter and a musicologist. While fulfilling these wonderful roles, it was perhaps inevitable that I should develop personal friendships with many of the stars whom I later employed when I launched Greshstyle Personal Appearances.

Not that all my earlier career moves were meticulously planned! After being sacked by my local record shop for taking the job as stand-in for Tom Courtenay in the film *Billy Liar*, I was promptly fired when Courtenay read the local press story of how I had got the job. I had told the papers I was to be the stand-in for Tom, and when Tom heard about my description he told me he would fire me if the story appeared. The story appeared in the local paper, and I found myself unemployed.

Undaunted, I went on to other ventures – and if you look very closely at an early episode of *Coronation Street*, broadcast in October 1963, you might just catch a glimpse of me when I played Jerry Booth's cycling club mate!

It was the early '60s when I launched my exclusive celebrity personal appearance booking agency: I arranged everything from booking the star to the production of posters and merchandise, such as the autographed pictures – 'Greshpics' as I called them, that were handed out at the events. Cayton Bay Holiday Camp always made a small charge for these pictures, usually 6*d*, which was donated to a local charity. I recall one occasion when Woolworth's booked thirty-six celebrities to appear in thirty-six different stores throughout the UK, and all on one day. I had to dig deep for that job – where on earth would I find so many star names available at one time? – but I managed it!

My client list read like a who's who of TV and film stars of the '70s: Tony Curtis, Peter Wyngarde, Dennis Waterman, Pat Phoenix, Violet Carson, Gordon Jackson, Hughie Green, Ken Dodd, Morecambe and Wise, and probably one of the most unusual 'celebrities', John Robert Russell, the 13th Duke of Bedford.

The celebrities who appeared reflected a who's who of the day's TV programmes: I regularly used the stars of the soap operas. From *Coronation Street* there were Gordon Kaye, Graham Haberfield, Irene Sutcliffe, Bernard Youens, Jean Alexander, Pat Phoenix, Violet Carson, Eileen Derbyshire, Margot Bryant and Doris Speed. From *Emmerdale Farm,* as it was known in the early days, there were Frazer Hines, Clive Hornby and Sheila Mercier. William Gaunt from *The Champions* was another; then there were TV announcer David Hamilton and radio presenters Alan Freeman and Pete Murray.

A lot of these actors and personalities were looking for an extra source of income and were happy to open supermarkets and bingo halls and meet 'their public'. One of the greatest crowd pleasers, particularly for the women, was Peter Wyngarde who played Jason King in the TV drama series. Peter always drew massive crowds and keeping them under control was a massive headache for me and my Gresh-team, but we always rose to the occasion!

Some of the organisations that used my services were Woolworth's and Fine Fare supermarkets, both sadly no longer on our high street, Ladbrokes and Top Rank Bingo clubs and Wallis's Holiday Camp at Cayton Bay, Scarborough. We also had carnival and shop openings to arrange. Wallis's was a particular favourite of many of my clients, who were booked over the summer season. Every Wednesday they had a 'come and meet' evening, when celebrities came to meet the campers. Who was booked was always kept a secret, which occasionally brought disappointment to some of the holidaymakers.

There is a tried and tested formula to hosting these events. Detail and timing is all important and I had the celebrities arrive in the store about five minutes late, which increased the tension in the crowd. The compère, who on many occasions was my close friend Garth Cawood, announced their arrival to the waiting crowds and escorted them to a suitably placed chair and table, where they would hand out the pre-signed pictures, the 'Greshpics'. These appearances usually lasted around forty-five minutes, or at least until the last picture had been handed out, and then it was off to the manager's office to meet staff and have photographs taken. It never ceased to amaze me the influence the managers' wives had on these proceedings. I was often asked to supply specific artists and when asked why was told 'My wife wants to meet them'. Everything was run like a military operation. When the event was over I got the celebrity back to the car and to the station or wherever they needed to be.

My agency was very successful, but I finally decided to close it down in 2003 to concentrate on the merchandise business that had been steadily growing for the last few years. I supplied personalised and promotional products for pantomimes and TV shows, which culminated in the ubiquitous foam 'Boo' hands we see today for children to wave at the baddies in the theatre and for Brian Dixon's Superslam Wrestling Promotions™. Someone has to provide them; children expect it now!

Whereby it is agreed

1. This Contract shall incorporate the Heads of Agreement of 2nd April, 1962 between British Actors' Equity Association and the Company (hereinafter called 'the Agreement').

2. ENGAGEMENT

   The Company hereby engages the Artist, who hereby accepts the engagement as under for the Artist's appearance in _CORONATION STREET Ep. 298_ as _Harrier_

   Intended Transmission Date(s) _21st October 1963_

   N.B. The Company is not bound to transmit the Artist's performance on such dates or at all.

	FEE	DATE	TIME	PLACE
3 (a) REHEARSALS (excluding performance days, recorded, filmed inserts and pre-recording of sound only days)	£2 2 0 per day from	16-18.10.63	as called	TV Centre, Manchester.
(b) PERFORMANCE (hereinafter called 'performance fee') Transmission Area: North	£7.7.0d.	18.10.63 V.T.R.	as arranged	TV Centre, Manchester.
(c) Pre-synching ~~RECORDED INSERTS~~	£5.5.0d.	16.10.63	1530 -1600	TV Centre, Manchester.
FILMED INSERTS	£			
TRAILERS	£			
DUMMY RUNS	£			

4. ADDITIONAL FEES for additional Transmission Rights:

   (a) *First Transmission:*   AREA: London   100% of the Performance Fee

                                      Midlands   100% of the Performance Fee

   Delete area covered by   ~~North~~   ~~100% of the Performance Fee~~

   Performance Fee   All Other Regions   100% of the Performance Fee

   (b) *Second Transmission:*

   (i) between 7.30 pm and 10 pm: 100% of the Performance Fee for each transmission area.

   (ii) before 7.30 pm or after 10 pm: 75% of the Performance Fee for each transmission area.

5. The Company guarantee payment of all the additional fees provided in Clause 4 (a) hereof, amounting with the Performance Fee to:

   (*This clause must be completed or deleted*)   £29.8.0d.

6. Travel and Subsistence ....

7. Billing   Mr Carl Gresham

SUBJECT TO ADDITIONAL PROVISIONS OVERLEAF

I accept the Engagement on   I accept the Engagement on the terms herein
the terms herein contained.   contained in respect of Overseas Use.

Coronation Street contract.

Coronation Street production still – spot The Gresh!

Kathy Staff on the set at Granada.

During this time I remained a freelance broadcaster and presenter joining Pennine Radio in Bradford where I presented a Sunday night show for many years. One of the highlights of this show was my series 'an hour in the company of', when I interviewed many of the celebrities I had worked with over the years.

From Pennine Radio I moved to Radio Aire, joining my colleague and now BBC local news presenter Christa Ackroyd, who had just become managing director, where I presented a similar show called *Relax and Remember* for many years on a Sunday evening. This was a lonely spot because at that time there was rarely anyone else in the studio. I can already hear you asking the question, 'What do you do when you want to go to the loo?' You put on the longest record you can find and off you go. On one occasion I chose the Rod Stewart song 'Sailing' and off I went. To my horror I heard on the station's internal speaker system that the record had got stuck! All the listeners would have known where I had been so I apologised on air, and said I had just been for a 'whisper'; then, as an afterthought, I said it was a good job I didn't need a shout! Live radio: you can't beat it.

Then I became the subject of an interview for the recently set up Bradford community radio station BCB 106.6FM, and was asked if I would like to host my own show. I still do to this day, once again inviting guests and friends from the world of stage and screen along with local celebrities and friends and anyone I think will interest my listeners.

Working on the radio show has allowed me to continue to bring old friends back to the studio, Frazer Hines is a regular, along with magician Paul Daniels and his wife Debbie McGee, legendary rocker Bill Wyman of the Rolling Stones, Mike Winters of Mike and Bernie Winters fame, comedians Jimmy Cricket and Billy Pearce, Con Cluskey of The Bachelors, actor and comedian Ricky Tomlinson, Roy Hudd, Ken Kitson, the policeman in *Last of the Summer Wine*, Graham 'Grumbleweed' Walker, soul legend Tommy Hunt . . . and so the list goes on. I also like to invite local celebrities to the show, such as Derek Lister, friend and author, Garth Cawood, who used to compère for me in the PA days, local musicians like Sammy King and Richard Harding, and local author and publisher Reuben Davison who has helped me get this autobiography together. You can hear my show on live on Sunday mornings on BCB Radio 106.6FM or via the internet, repeated on Mondays and Tuesdays. Sadly for me the cricket gets in the way during the summer, so I lose the live Sunday morning show.

Most of the people I have worked with have been a delight; those that weren't haven't been named, either because I don't want any legal issues or simply because I would prefer to remember only the good ones.

While I only worked with some of the celebrities once, many appeared with me over and over again, and I made friendships that have lasted to this day. I have included pictures as well as the written word because it's sometimes difficult to picture a name. I hope you enjoy the nostalgic trip down memory lane as much as I have compiling it; it's brought back many happy memories for me and I hope it will for you too.

An early photo of Helen and The Gresh.

(facing page) The Gresh in costume.

Laurence Oliver founded a fan club in JEAN ALEXANDER's honour: the British League for Hilda Ogden.

People, Places, Events

Jean Alexander
Who could forget Hilda and Stan Ogden in *Coronation Street*? Jean played the part for years. She wasn't comfortable with the appearance circuit and was always reluctant to have a go. It was only through Bernard Youens, her on-screen husband, that I finally managed to persuade her to appear at Cayton Bay Holiday Camp. Jean was a great actress, not just a soap star, and didn't much like the high life that actresses like Pat Phoenix aspired to. She tolerated Pat and her constant headline-grabbing life and just got on with the job of playing Hilda Ogden.

Jean once told me a story that sums up how the public see these soap stars. She was on a cruise, dressed in all her finery, having just played Auntie Wainwright in *Last of the Summer Wine*. She overheard two ladies say, 'I told you it was Hilda Ogden. You'd recognise her anywhere.'

Alexandra Bastedo
Alexandra Bastedo was probably best known for her role as Sharron Macready in *The Champions*, alongside fellow actors William Gaunt (Richard Barrett) and Stuart Damon (Craig Stirling), which came to British televisions in 1968.

The series that shot her to fame in the UK revolved around the fictitious United Nations organisation Nemesis. Alexandra's role was that of a recently widowed doctor and scientist. On the team's first mission their plane crashes in the Himalayas and they are rescued by an advanced civilisation, living in secret, who save them and give them enhanced powers to communicate by telepathy and to foresee the future.

I managed to get Alexandra to appear at Wallis's Holiday Camp near Scarborough in 1969, at the request of the company boss Dudley Wallis. Dudley was a stickler for detail: I remember once receiving a bill sent directly

 ALEXANDRA BASTEDO has run an animal sanctuary for twenty-five years, and records her experiences in her book *Beware, Dobermans, Donkeys and Ducks.*

from his office for 'fresh strawberries supplied to the Gresh party'. I queried the bill with Dudley, only to be told that he had agreed to pay for afternoon tea, not for any extras.

Dudley was keen to meet Alexandra, and told me that he would confirm the next year's contract if I could get her to appear. This was an opportunity too good to miss. In fact many of the celebrities I booked were at his personal request: I suppose that as it was his business he could decide who to have. There have to be benefits of being the boss!

Alexandra drew the biggest crowd we had ever seen. In just one hour over a thousand people queued to see her and get a signed photo. We always had them pre-signed because there simply wasn't time to have each one individually done.

I was fortunate to meet and have lunch with her a couple of years ago and she is still as beautiful as ever.

One of Dudley's strangest requests was for the aviator Sheila Scott OBE. At the time I was trying to convince him to get the actor Sam Kydd, who had appeared in numerous films and TV programmes; he was willing to do these appearances and I thought he would be a much bigger draw. No, Dudley wanted Sheila and Sheila he got, much to the guests' disappointment that week. They were all extremely courteous, but wondering why last week they had had Pat Phoenix from *Coronation Street* and next week they had Alexandra Bastedo from *The Champions*.

Batley Variety Club

I was lucky enough to meet film star Jayne Mansfield while I was working as Press Relations Officer at the Batley Variety Club in West Yorkshire. Batley Variety Club was a major venue in the seventies with artists from all over the world performing on their stage. Jayne, better known for her films, had a rather dreadful cabaret act, but meeting her in the flesh, so to speak, was a real thrill. And I have the photographs to prove it. I was the envy of many male colleagues at the time.

I was also fortunate to meet The Big 'O', Roy Orbison.

Sadly, Batley Variety Club no longer exists; cabaret clubs declined rapidly during the early '80s across the whole country. In Yorkshire alone we had two of the finest clubs with Batley and the Wakefield Theatre Club, both of which attracted the biggest names of the day.

Tony Blackburn

Legendary Radio 1 presenter and one of my hardest-working clients, Tony was at the height of his success when we were working together, presenting the breakfast show on Radio 1 and *Top of the Pops* on television every week. While I booked him to open some stores, he was happiest visiting discos around the country. On some nights we visited two or three, repeating it the following evening, always drawing a massive sell-out crowd. He once commented to me that my name appeared more times on the publicity hand-outs than his own, which might have been true. In fact it *was* true.

(left) With Brenda Lee.

(below) With the big 'O' - Roy Orbison.

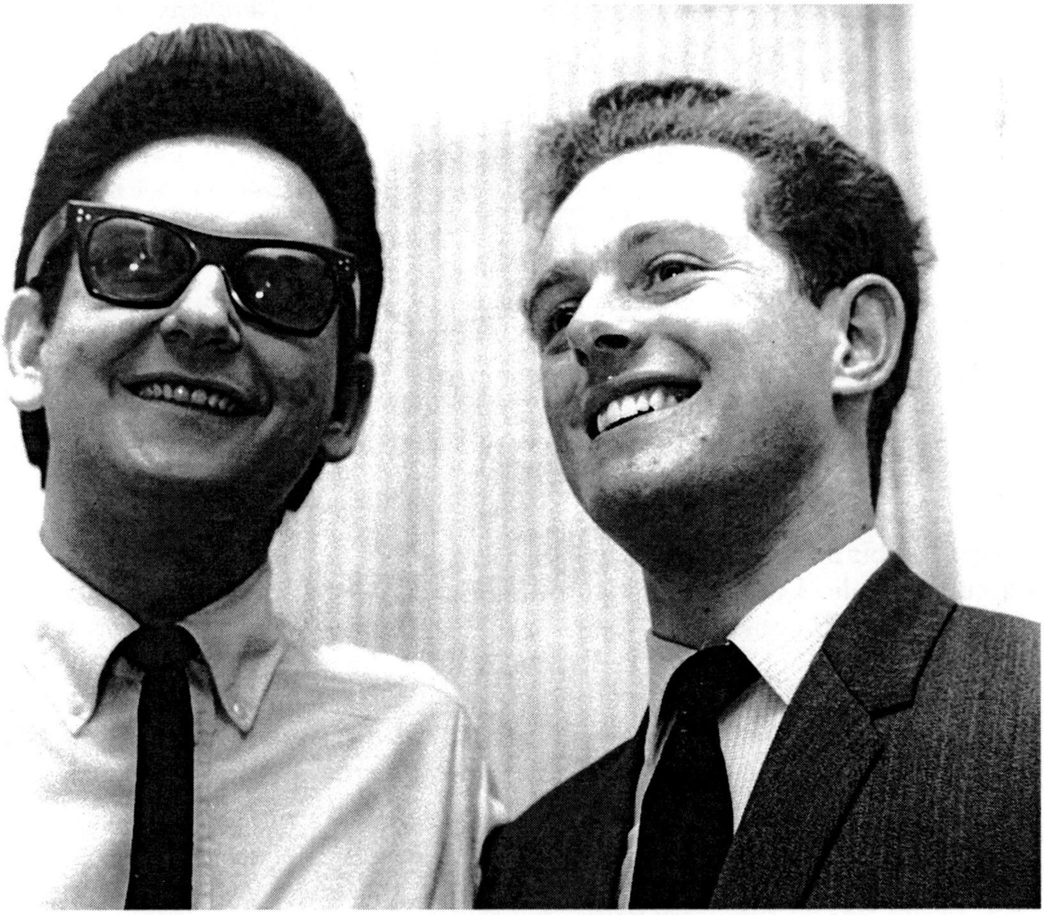

With Jayne Mansfield.

Margot Bryant

Who could forget Minnie Caldwell in *Coronation Street?* Alongside Ena Sharples (Violet Carson) she was a stalwart of the series, sitting in the snug at the Rovers Return for many years. While a delightful woman to work with and very modest, never quite understanding why people wanted to meet her and get her autograph, she could be quite a snob. I remember on one occasion going to pick her up from her flat in Manchester and she asked me if the people she was meeting would be able to appreciate her fine clothes. Perhaps they wouldn't have seen such quality, she said. I was stunned. She always seemed a gentle, timid lady, and this comment was quite out of character. Out of character maybe, but the real Margot Bryant.

According to Jean Alexander's autobiography, MARGOT BRYANT had a wide and surprising vocabulary of four letter words!

Violet Carson

Ena Sharples in *Coronation Street*, and what a character in real life. I suppose the two leading ladies of *The Street* were Violet and Pat Phoenix, who played Elsie Tanner. I adored Pat and became close friends with her over many years, but got caught up in their off-screen battles over who was the more famous and particularly who would be paid the most. This battle came to a head during an appearance at Wallis's Cayton Bay Holiday Camp. Violet told me she had been speaking to Pat, who said she was earning £100. Pat was always my highest paid client – but she was only earning £75, in those days a sizeable fee. Violet told me she wanted 100 guineas, not pounds, before she would sign a contract: she had to earn more than Pat. Pat had a tendency to promote herself among other cast members; she tended to exaggerate her worth, you might say. This made it very difficult for me on several occasions when I was negotiating fees with other cast members.

Violet was nothing like her character in real life. She was an excellent pianist, but would never play at the events I booked her for, despite many requests. I always had to be careful when using the *Coronation Street* stars because the rivalry was so intense between them. Other *Coronation Street* characters I worked with were Doris Speed, better known as Annie Walker, owner of the Rovers Return, and her on-screen husband Jack Walker, Arthur Leslie, who made a few appearances at the Majorca Holiday Centre for me as well.

Some of the other actors you might remember were Irene Sutcliffe (who played Maggie Clegg), Sandra Gough (who played Irma Barlow and Irma Ogden) and, still going strong to this day, Johnny Briggs – best known as Mike Baldwin.

VIOLET CARSON was originally a pianist for silent movies, and often appeared on the radio from the mid-1930s. She was Wilfrid Pickles's piano player on his long-running *Have A Go* programme. One of her programmes was billed in the *Radio Times* as *Songs at the Piano – with Violent Carson*.

Roy Castle

Roy appeared for me at one of the Top Rank Bingo Clubs. As he was an all-round entertainer I thought he would go down well at the club. His normal cabaret act lasted around an hour and a half. When we got to the venue he was told that bingo was the most important thing, and he wasn't needed for any more than half an hour: the same rule applied to any of the stars they invited.

I remember Roy coughing a lot even then, and it was sad to hear of his death from lung cancer – which many thought was the result of smoky atmospheres in all the clubs and venues he'd worked at throughout his career.

Judith Chalmers

I booked Judith on a number of occasions. She presented a number of programmes on TV, including the hugely popular series *Come Dancing*, and was to be seen regularly commentating on fashion and the like from Ascot and Henley Regatta. Later she was best known for presenting the travel show *Wish You Were Here*.

One of our appearances ended up taking the whole day rather than the usual couple of hours. Judith had been asked to open the Tarporley Carnival in Cheshire. On arrival a committee member asked if she would judge the baby show and then the fancy dress competition, and if that wasn't enough would she crown the Carnival Queen? On top of that the committee had decided to charge for the signed photos we handed out. Talk about getting your money's worth! But as ever Judith was charming and carried out all the requests. That turned out to be another of those exceptionally long days.

In 2008 JUDITH CHALMERS said, to Graham Norton, 'I'm sorry to reveal that after thirty years of *Wish You Were Here*, I was pantless all the time.' A wardrobe assistant had told her that this was the only way to avoid a 'visible panty line' on TV.

Coronation Street

Booking one celebrity can be difficult and many don't want to appear with others, but I think I set a record when I was asked to book *Coronation Street* stars to open a gift shop in Newcastle. For that event I think I managed to book most of the cast. We had Jack Howarth, who played Albert Tatlock, Alan Browning, who played Alan Howard and later went on to marry Pat Phoenix, Doris Speed, who was Annie Walker, and finally Eileen Derbyshire, who played Miss Nugent. This could have been a recipe for disaster; so many actors from the one show in one place at one time. It wasn't. They were all brilliant, and the crowd loved having them all together.

JACK HOWARTH – *Coronation Street*'s Albert Tatlock – received an MBE in 1983 for his charity work.

Tony Curtis

When Tony Curtis appeared in *The Persuaders*, British actor Reginald Marsh, often to be seen playing Dave Smith in *Coronation Street* and who worked for me on many occasions, was also part of the cast – although only for one episode. Tony had been enquiring about earning some extra income while he was in Britain, and Reginald suggested he contacted me about personal appearances. I was duly summoned to London to meet Tony at the house where he was staying – which just happened to be Shirley Bassey's. She was away at the time so unfortunately I didn't get to meet her on this occasion (although I had met her while I was working as press officer at Batley Variety Club). Obviously I was very keen to get Tony Curtis on my books, but we never managed to find dates that were suitable for him. I have numerous letters that he sent me, but we never finalised anything, something I have always regretted. It wasn't for want of trying, I can assure you.

Stuart Damon

One of Alexandra Bastedo's co-stars in *The Champions* alongside William Gaunt was Stuart Damon, a very handsome American actor who proved very popular on the appearance circuit. Just like Peter Wyngarde he was a great hit with the ladies. While he was best known for his TV show he wanted to try his hand at singing, and asked me to try to find him some engagements at clubs. The Batley Variety Club was the best known in the North of England

STUART DAMON's parents were Russian Jewish immigrants, who made their home in America after fleeing the Bolshevik Revolution.

The Champions: left to right, Alexandra Bastedo, Stuart Damon and William Gaunt.

and attracted artists from all over the world, so I suggested we tried there. Stuart said that if I managed to get him a booking at Batley I could manage him permanently: another challenge for The Gresh, and I rose to it. I got him that booking – and many more, and his singing career started to take off. This led to one of the most unusual journeys I have ever had to take with one of my clients.

I was used to driving from one end of the country to the other, week in and week out, but not quite so used to trips to South America, Bogota in Colombia to be precise. They held a song festival there, and Stuart was invited to attend. We did the festival and Stuart, being American, wanted to visit the States before returning to Britain. As this wasn't part of the travel plans we managed to get flights to Miami, where he could go off and make the visits he wanted to. Not having planned this little jaunt I didn't have a visa, so I should have stayed in the airport, but I didn't. I took a short trip into the city, and unfortunately missed my flight as it was called two hours earlier than I had expected. A very embarrassing confrontation with Customs officials ensued, and I was given a stern warning never to do it again.

With Alexandra Bastedo.

Ken Dodd

Another of my legendary clients, Ken was famous for his 'diddymen'. Similar to Snow White's seven dwarfs, they were an integral part of his act and I supplied him with merchandise for his shows. The hardest part of working with him was his poor time-keeping. He quite happily arrived at the venue late, confident in the knowledge that the crowd would be waiting however long it took. No one was going to rush Ken Dodd. He was always a stickler for the money side; you may remember his court case over unpaid taxes. He has managed to include references to that in his act ever since. He once said to me that tax was a penny in the pound when he was a lad, and he thought it still was!

Ken may have arrived late but you got your money's worth when he finally did appear. He could quite easily over run his scheduled appearance by an hour or more if he was having fun, and still does to this day. While the audience love it, many theatre venues become exasperated as they have to keep staff and musicians, if there is an orchestra, on overtime.

During the 1960s KEN DODD told 1,500 jokes in three and a half hours at a Liverpool theatre, a feat that gained him a place in the *Guinness Book of Records*.

Clive Dunn

Everyone seemed to love Clive. He is probably most famous for his role in *Dad's Army* as the bumbling Corporal Jones with his catchphrases of 'Don't panic' and 'They don't like it up 'em'. He was always an entertainer, and I particularly remember one night in Leeds. I had taken him back to the station to catch his train back home when it was announced that there would be a delay. I was disappointed, and said I would stay with him until it finally arrived. What a wait I had. Clive proceeded to work his way through his entire cabaret act, there on the platform of Leeds station, for me and a few others who had gathered round.

Dick Emery

Another TV star whom the public loved to meet, Dick was always keen to work for me, but had one stipulation in his contract. His fee was always to be paid in cash before his appearance. I hasten to add that this wasn't for any underhand reason: he simply liked to see his fee and know that all had been settled before he did his bit.

DICK EMERY was chairman of the Airfix Modellers' Club. As well as model-making, his hobbies included aviation and motorcycling.

Bruce Forsyth

Bruce always was, and still is, a very busy man, which made it very difficult to get hold of him for appearances. As the star of *The Generation Game*, he was at the height of his TV career when I managed to book him in 1977 to open a new Ladbrokes casino in Halifax, West Yorkshire. The management of Ladbrokes had laid down a bit of a challenge, as they had said they wanted three particular TV stars of the day: Bruce Forsyth, Derek Batey, presenter of the game show *Mr and Mrs* and John Inman, star of the popular sitcom *Are You Being Served?* Yes, you guessed it, I got the lot. Bruce only worked for me once, but I rose to that challenge!

BRUCE FORSYTH has twice been voted the Greatest UK Game Show Host of All Time, in 2002 and 2006. There is a bronze bust of him at the London Palladium.

Alan Freeman

Alan Freeman, Radio I DJ, was another personality who I became good friends with. Our initial meeting didn't get off to a good start. Ever the gentleman and professional, he said he would come up a day earlier for an appearance I had organised, so we could have a night out and do the appearance the following day; he would then stay over with me in the evening and return home the following morning. He said he would sort out his own hotel because he didn't expect me to pay for it. I was amazed: most of the people I worked with expected everything to be paid for, without question.

Alan rang back a little while later to say he had booked the 'so and so' hotel. I didn't recognise the name. I asked him to repeat the name, and he said the 'so and so' hotel in Bedford. I said, 'No, it's Bradford you're coming to: the appearance is at Cayton Bay Holiday Camp in Scarborough.' That was a close call, but we got it sorted and ended up in the right place. Maybe there was a lesson in this, to book all my guests' accommodation myself, however considerate they thought they were being.

Alan and I managed to cover a lot of disco openings and appearances in our time together. I was privileged to attend a party with him where the guests included The Beatles, Alma Cogan and Alan's fellow DJ Tony Blackburn. Alan gave me one piece of advice that I have never forgotten: he said, 'Use your voice to introduce the talent; you're not more talented.'

ALAN FREEMAN was nicknamed 'Fluff' because of a favourite jumper that he wore until it was covered in fluff balls.

With Alan Freeman.

In 1975 THE GOODIES released five hit singles, all of them written by Bill Oddie.

The Goodies

I had many requests to book Tim Brooke-Taylor, Graeme Garden and Bill Oddie, collectively known as The Goodies, but only managed it once for the opening of a Fine Fare supermarket in Blackpool in 1979. I was so impressed with them that I produced individual photo-cards for them rather than a single one. They were some of the longest biographies I had ever done as they had all achieved so much in their careers. We stayed over in Blackpool the previous night and had a wonderful time. The crowds were enormous when we arrived at the supermarket and they proved extremely popular. I tried many times to get them booked again, but never managed it, much to the disappointment of many clients.

DAVID HAMILTON was born David Pilditch. He adopted his mother's maiden name when he went into showbusiness.

David Hamilton

David is a great friend, and was kind enough to write the foreword for this book. We worked a lot together as David was keen on the PA scene and found it very rewarding, quite literally. He became well known as a continuity announcer on what was then ATV, later to become Granada television. He also hosted his own Radio 1 show for many years. You may remember his nickname, 'Diddy' David Hamilton. This came from Ken Dodd, who christened him following some work they did together. David and I worked extremely hard doing the PAs, sometimes completing three a day before I had to get him back to the studio for his real job. Our best performance was four galas in one day. It drained both of us, but we did it.

Larry Grayson

Larry was well known for hosting the *Generation Game* along with Isla St Clair, who incidentally also worked for me, opening a new Fine Fare store in Hartlepool. Camp is probably the best word to describe him; he was perhaps not always to everyone's taste. However, catchphrases are always popular, and who can forget Larry's 'shut that door', along with too many others to repeat here. We

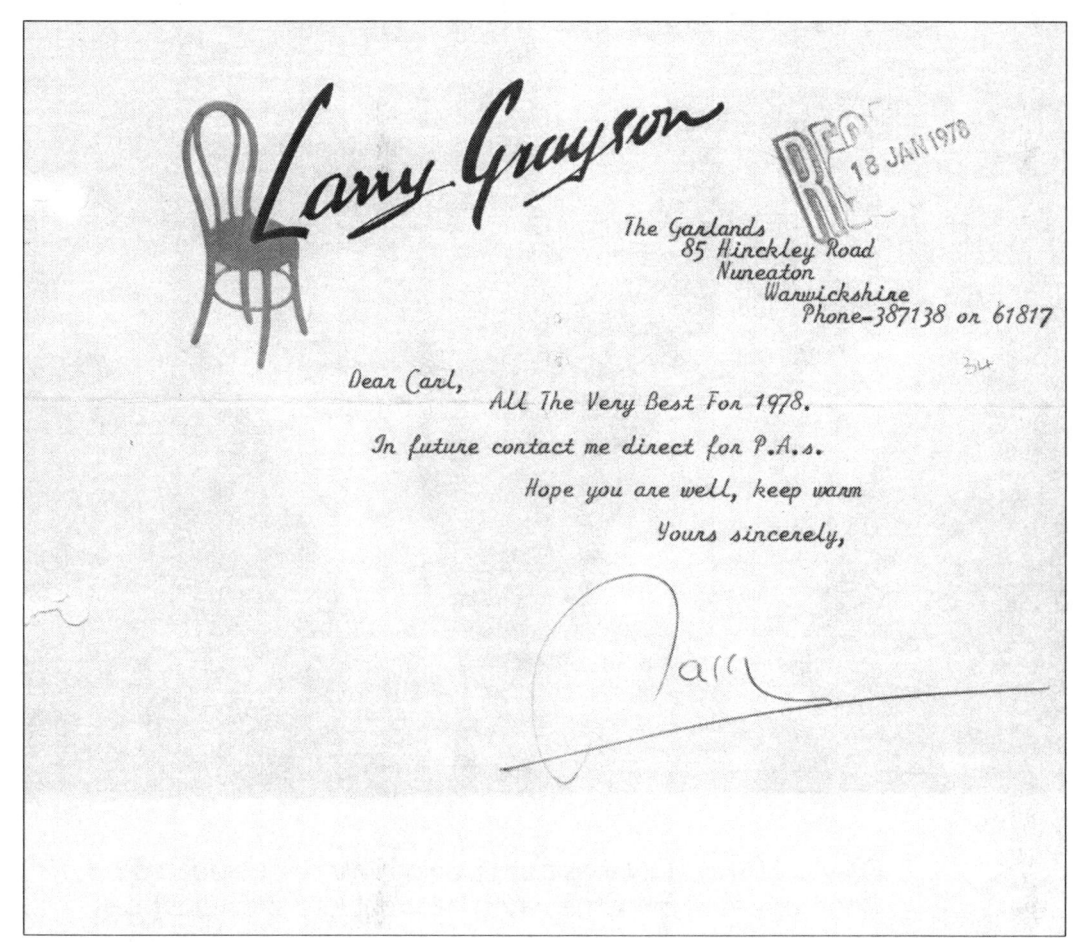

LARRY GRAYSON's characters, Slack Alice, Apricot Lil, Pop-It-In-Pete, Self-Raising Fred and all, were based on real people. His last words were his catchphrase 'Shut that door!'

worked together many times: he was very much in demand with the public and with my clients as he was at the height of his TV popularity.

Not only was Larry extremely popular with the public, he was one of my all-time favourite celebrities to work with and a favourite of my partner Helen. I remember one occasion when we went to see him at his home in Nuneaton. Unknown to Helen, I had also booked tickets for us to see Diana Ross at the Birmingham NEC.

When we arrived, Larry surprised us by saying, 'Would you like to see my new car?' He took us to his garage and proudly showed us a brand new Rolls-Royce convertible. Helen was fascinated and suggested we should all go for a drive. I still hadn't told her I had tickets for Diana Ross at the NEC, and time was running short. And another problem: Larry didn't drive, and I certainly didn't want to be responsible for driving a car of that cost and quality, which left Helen. So she drove, quite happily. I didn't want to spoil the afternoon, but in a private moment I managed to explain my dilemma to Larry, and he saved the day by telling Helen he had friends arriving soon and had to get back. Helen still didn't know about the concert, but when we left Larry's home I pulled over and said that even though I knew she would have loved to have stayed, and we would have been very welcome, I had other plans for us. Then I got out the Diana Ross tickets. Despite Helen's disappointment at not being able to spend more time with Larry she enjoyed the concert, and my plans came together nicely.

Hughie Green
I have so many stories and memories about this TV legend. Hughie and I became close friends during the time we worked together, which made life all the more enjoyable.

Hughie is best known for *Double Your Money* and *Opportunity Knocks*, but he wasn't always a TV host: he had appeared in a few films such as *Mr Midshipman Easy*, *Tom Brown's Schooldays* and *Hills of Home*. Hughie also held a pilot's licence from his days as a flight lieutenant.

Always one of my most popular celebrities on the PA circuit, Hughie was a particular favourite with the Woolworth stores management. We ended up doing many appearances for them over the years.

There are two stories I must recount.

It was 1970, and Hughie and I had had a very busy day in Scotland opening a Woolworth store in Glasgow, then a garden centre in Edinburgh and finally a new bingo hall back in Glasgow. As Hughie had to be back in London the following day we decided to get the train back from Glasgow. Hughie had asked me if I would like to attend a recording of his *Opportunity Knocks* show. It was late and we were both relaxing when a very smart gentleman arrived in our compartment. He explained that he was the Chief Security Officer for the then Prime Minister, Harold Wilson, who was also on the train. The Prime Minister had found out Hughie was travelling and had expressed a desire to meet him. So

During the Second World War HUGHIE GREEN was in the Royal Canadian Air Force and ferried aeroplanes across the Atlantic; he still worked as a charter pilot even at the height of his success as an entertainer.

"FRIENDS, IT'S GREAT TO SEE YOU'VE FOUND A WAY TO BEAT THE NEW POSTAL CHARGES."

off we went to chat to Harold Wilson! We all chatted for quite some time about Yorkshire and Harold Wilson's friendship with Lord Kagan, he of the Gannex raincoat that Harold was famous for wearing and was manufactured near Halifax in West Yorkshire. As we were leaving Harold suggested that we should visit No. 10 for drinks sometime. Now there was an invitation not to be missed.

Hughie and I got back to his flat and collected his car to make the journey to Teddington Lock studios where *Opportunity Knocks* was recorded. I started to jot down a short note to thank the Prime Minister for the invitation and to try to sort out a date. Hughie was appalled, and told me to stop writing immediately. No way was I to write: if Harold Wilson wanted to invite us he knew where to find us, through Hughie of course. Needless to say I never saw an invitation, and never got to have drinks at No. 10.

My next story describes what was something of a controversy at the time. *Opportunity Knocks* was for new talent, certainly not people who had already got careers or had careers, which was why our visit to a club in Brighouse, West Yorkshire was so unusual. We had just finished an appearance at a bingo hall in Huddersfield when Hughie noticed that singer P.J. Proby was appearing at the club we were passing. I couldn't understand why Hughie was so keen to see him. Proby had been a massive star in the UK as well as America and there wasn't any

THAMES 'Opportunity Knocks'

1. I/WE __JAMES MARCUS SMITH__ (full name) apply to be and Stage Name auditioned for the Thames Television Programme, 'Opportunity Knocks.'
2. Address __3, The Textile Hall, Aldams Road, Dewsbury,__ __West Yorkshire.__ Telephone Home __N/A__
3. Age __Over 21__ Telephone/Business/Friend/Agent __N/A__
4. Type of Act __American Style Vocal Entertainer__
5. Details of Act and/or songs to be performed at the audition. __Strong deep vocal with interpretations of songs like 'I Apologise', 'The American Trilogy' and other popular items__
6. Previous experience.
   RADIO (Title & Date) __Some experience on local radio in The States__
   TELEVISION (Title & Date) __Some appearances many years ago__
   AUDITIONS (Title & Date) __Hundreds__
   CLUBS & CABARET (and for how long) __Usual Circuit of British Venues__
7. Normal Occupation. __Entertainer__

I undertake as follows:
(a) That I am a Citizen of the United Kingdom or the Republic of Ireland.
(b) That I am not under contract to any organisation or person who could prevent me from appearing or attach any condition to my appearing on television.
(c) To appear punctually for the audition, on the understanding that I may be disqualified should I be late.
(d) To be photographed before, during and after the audition and acknowledge that Thames Television Limited shall have the right to publish all such photographs in such manner as it may wish.
(e) That I apply for this audition at my own risk and will make no claim against Thames Television Limited or any other person, firm or company in respect of any personal injury or damage to or loss of property which I may suffer in attending the audition.
(f) That I shall not be entitled to the reimbursement of any expenses which I may incur in attending the audition.
(g) That my act will not last longer than three minutes.
(h) That I will provide all props and musical instruments required for my act (except piano).
(i) That I will provide my own sheet music should I do an act that requires piano accompaniment.

I understand that:
(j) If successful at the audition, I will be notified in writing within three weeks, and that the decision of the audition panel is final and no correspondence can be entered into.
(k) Neither Thames Television nor Hughie Green guarantees that I will appear on television even if successful at the audition, and even if actually called for a programme.
I certify that the above information concerning myself is correct to the best of my knowledge and belief and that I have read the rules for the 'Opportunity Knocks' programme overleaf, and agree to abide by them.

Signed _James Marcus Smith_ Date __29th July 1977__
Note

Contract for the masked P.J. Proby.

reason for Hughie to be taking an interest, but he was determined. 'Let's go see him, Golden Balls,' he said. Golden Balls was his nickname for me, why I don't know; I used to call him God. So in we went and caught the last thirty minutes of the act. Hughie went backstage after the show and spoke to Proby, to my horror and utter dismay suggesting that he might like a crack at the show. I was gobsmacked. Proby's career had been on the wane for quite some time, and Hughie wanted to give him another chance. This simply wasn't allowed and the Thames Television bosses would have been horrified if they had known what Hughie was planning.

P.J. Proby, 'The Masked Singer' as viewers saw him.

Hughie decided that it would be best if Proby filled in the application form under his real name, James Marcus Smith, and appeared as 'The Masked Singer', to disguise who he really was. His contract was given to me for safe-keeping, even though I had nothing to do with the show. One of the executives rang me to get some background on this guy; needless to say I couldn't say much, nor did I want to!

When P.J. Proby turned up for rehearsals Bob Sharples, the band leader for *Opportunity Knocks*, recognised him immediately, as did most of the band. They all kept quiet, however, and began rehearsals. 'The Masked Singer' performed 'American Trilogy', and it was fantastic. Everyone agreed he was going to be the winner with a performance like that. But it all went horribly wrong. He had a girl with him on the show night, and whether she or someone else smuggled booze into his dressing room I don't know, but by the time he came to do his spot he was paralytic; he could hardly stand. And someone had tipped off the newspapers so we had journalists all over the studio. Sadly he sounded awful and came last, which was no surprise to anyone. The papers had a field day with the story, and the débâcle resulted in Thames cancelling any further series of *Opportunity Knocks* and thereby ending Hughie's career.

You can't take away Hughie's influence on variety TV of the time: he was responsible for the early careers of many popular stars. Why he took this chance I don't know. I suppose the modern equivalent of Hughie is Simon Cowell on *Britain's Got Talent*.

```
                                POST  OFFICE               No. 247
 Charges to pay                                            OFFICE STAMP
  Tariff  £                     TELEGRAM
  V.A.T. £         Prefix.  Time handed in.  Office of origin and Service Instructions.  Words.
  Total  £
                                                            At_____ m
  ..CEIVED
  From _____  ＊M181 5.0 LONDON T SW 46                    To_____
  By   [sig]                                                By_____

       = THE KOREA GUIDERS AGENCY SUITE SEVEN THE
       TEXTILE HALL ALDAMS RD DEWSBURY-YKS =
       ATTENTION KOREA GUIDERS AGENCY STOP WHY DONT YO
       GET ONE STOP SORRY TO SEE WHITFIELD HAS COMMITT
       PROFESSIONAL SUICIDE BY JOINING YOUR MULTIFARIOUS
       ORGANISATION STOP = ONE OF YOUR MANY ENEMIES
                 H GREEN 01-486 3136

       For free repetit  +++01-486 3136 +   TSG TGMS LNES       B or C
       at office of deliv
```

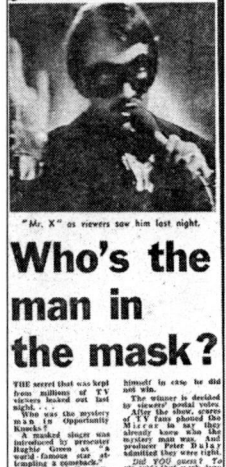

Memories of Hughie Green.

News of the World FEB 12 1978.

'SACKED' HUGHIE THREATENS: I'LL BASH UP ITV BOSSES

By STEVE BISHOP

HUGHIE GREEN'S Opportunity Knocks talent show could be a real knockout when it goes on the air for the last time next month.

Not only is Hughie hoping to present a cast of stars he has discovered. He is also threaten-

HUGHIE GREEN

169, Chiltern Court,
Baker Street,
London,
NW1 5SW.

28th October, 1975.

Carl Gresham, Esq.,
235 Pennine Radio,
P.O. Box 235,
Pennine House,
Forster Square,
Bradford, BD1 5NP.

Dear Mr. Gresham,

As I deal with Mr. Green's engagements, I am replying to your letter dated 22nd October on his behalf.

Mr. Green was overwhelmed to receive your invitation to be your very first <u>special guest</u> on a chat programme lasting about One Hour in total. However, in order to give your personal request the most sincerest consideration, and as you so quite rightly say Mr. Green is a very, very busy man, may I please draw to your attention the fact that you unfortunately forget to mention the <u>special guest</u> fee that you are prepared to offer this very professional and much sought after man for his services.

I await your early reply.

Yours sincerely,

C. F. Rowe.

C.F. Rowe. (Mrs)
<u>Secretary to Hughie Green.</u>

Frazer Hines

One of the biggest TV soaps of the time was ITV's *Emmerdale Farm*. The cast were always in demand for events, and at some time or another most of them worked for me - including Arthur Pentelow who played Henry Wilkes, Sheila Mercier (Annie Sugden, mother of Frazer's character), Clive Hornby (Jack Sugden) and Katherine Barker, who played the original Dolly, later to be played by Jean Rogers. I also engaged Frederick Pyne, who played Matt, and Dolly Skillbeck. They had just married in the series and punters wanted to see the 'happy couple' together.

FRAZER HINES is a noted amateur jockey, and also owns an Australian record label – Red Disc Records.

Notices announcing Frazer's appearance - with his name misspelled.

One who was to become a close friend was Frazer Hines, who played Joe Sugden. We spent hours together driving to and from events, and we became very close.

Frazer's first wife was stage star Gemma Craven. While I organised appearances for Frazer, my partner Helen, who was a hairdresser, was asked to be Gemma's hairdresser for the run of *They're Playing Our Song*, which starred Tom Conti. The credit in the programme read 'Gemma's hair by Gresham', with no mention of Helen's name. I was extremely disappointed about this: I really wanted my beloved Helen to get full credit for her work; but it wasn't to be.

Frazer stayed at our home many times while he was filming *Emmerdale Farm*. Often he wandered round the house for a while, collected a book from my shelves and disappeared to the loo for half an hour. What a life I lead with the stars!

Sadly Frazer's marriage to Gemma ended in divorce. Helen and I found out Gemma was going to announce their split when Frazer was working in Pitlochry. He was devastated, and the papers said he had collapsed. Helen and I felt very protective towards him, and decided to drive up to Pitlochry to collect him. He was indeed in a bad way, and we immediately brought him back to our house in Bradford. Sadly, as both Gemma and Frazer were well known at the time the papers got involved, and Helen and I were fascinated to read a story in a Scottish paper that he had been found fishing in Scotland. Strange when he was in our house in Bradford!

Not long afterwards Frazer's character was written out of the series: they killed his character so there was no way back, which upset him. Other characters' departures had been left open.

One funny story I shall never forget is when Frazer turned up at my house before one of our events. I can't remember what car he had at the time, but it was rather posh. As I got in he asked what I did for Ronnie Maghill, who played Amos Brearley in *Emmerdale Farm*. I asked what he meant. Frazer said, 'You drive him to these events.' 'I know I do, but Ronnie can't drive so I have to.' At which point Frazer climbed out of his own car, got into mine and said, 'In that case just call *me* Ronnie.' So I was back to driving!

Frazer and I are good friends to this day, and we enjoy the occasional holiday together.

Mary Holland

Who? I hear you say. Mary was most famous for playing the mother in the TV commercial for Oxo in the '70s. She had appeared as Jenny in *Mrs Dale's Diary* and also had a part in the BBC series *Doomwatch* in the early '70s, but it was her role in the commercial that most people recognised her for.

My relationship with her sadly came to an end when I received a letter from the Oxo company requesting details of her engagements with me and asking what fee she was being paid. I informed them that I thought it was none of their business, and that if Mary wanted to tell them the details she could; I certainly wasn't going to. Sadly she became 'unavailable' thereafter. It was sad, because she was adored and had done a lot of appearances for me.

MARY HOLLAND appeared in the Oxo adverts for eighteen years from 1958; she and her husband, played by Richard Clarke, were replaced by humorous adverts featuring Dennis Waterman.

John Inman

John was another TV favourite, probably best known for his role in *Are You Being Served?* as the rather camp sales assistant Mr Humphries. John was another of the stars who had already worked their way up through theatre before hitting the big time on our TV screens. He appeared in musicals such as *Ann Veronica*, played the part of PC Boot in the record-breaking musical *Salad Days* on its national tour, and starred in *Charlie's Aunt* in the West End. John is also a keen panto performer, with a regular role as Mother Goose.

Through *Are You Being Served?* John appeared regularly on shows such as *Celebrity Squares*, *The Good Old Days* and – how many of you remember this one? – *Seaside Special*.

Record-breaking summer season runs in Blackpool were all part of John's career, but he was still keen on doing the PA circuit as he was much in demand. He was a firm favourite of the Ladbrokes bingo hall management, so we had many engagements across the UK. As I supplied the publicity cards for these

In later years JOHN INMAN appeared as a pantomime dame in more than forty productions.

appearances he eventually asked me to produce all his signed photographs, which led to one of the most bizarre journeys of my life. John rang one day to say he had run out of publicity shots, so could I organise some more as soon as possible. He was appearing at the Bristol Hippodrome at the time so I thought I had better drive down and get them straight to him. The printer rushed them through, I collected them and headed off. As I lived in and worked from Bradford it was a significant journey. My plan was to see John, give him the photos, see the show he was in (confident he would get me a ticket), stay over and drive back the following day.

I got down to the theatre, explained at the stage door who I was, found John and handed him the pictures, explaining that I had got them printed as fast as possible. John thanked me, then turned round and went back to his dressing room, leaving me standing there! I was stunned: there was no mention of a ticket to see the show, or acknowledgement of the fact that I had driven 300 miles to get them to him. I decided to return home straight away. It was a very long day.

Gordon Jackson
Gordon was another familiar face to TV viewers, Mr Hudson the butler in *Upstairs, Downstairs* and Cowley in *The Professionals* with Martin Shaw and Lewis Collins. I did a few events with Lewis Collins who insisted on bringing a bodyguard, which rather defeated the object when he was meant to be meeting the public. Martin Shaw was completely different, a pleasure to work with. He

Martin Shaw round at ours with Carol.

GORDON JACKSON was a draughtsman at Rolls-Royce after he left school aged fifteen, and his film career began when Ealing producers were looking for a young Scot for the 1942 film *The Foreman Went To France*.

enjoyed the personal appearances as much as the TV work. Helen and I had him to stay at our house before some events, which made the neighbours think we were running some kind of hotel for TV stars; they christened our road Celebrity Grove because of the number of stars we had visiting.

Gordon Jackson was such a modest man. He could never quite understand why so many people wanted to meet him. And I must say he was one of the most elegant men I have ever worked with. I remember him telling me about the occasion on which he was invited to Buckingham Palace for lunch. When he was shown in he was offered a glass of wine, which he refused as he was teetotal. He asked for a glass of milk instead – which gave the staff a minor problem. The kitchens were a long way from the reception room, and Gordon overheard one of the snooty, liveried servants say, 'He doesn't want wine, he wants ****ing milk!' Gordon said he had almost finished the first course before his milk arrived.

Yootha Joyce and Brian Murphy

I am putting Yootha and Brian together because that is how most people will remember them. They were the strange couple who lived in the downstairs flat in the TV series *Man About The House*, starring Richard O'Sullivan, Paula Wilcox and Sally Thomsett. Both of them had extensive theatrical careers before attaining stardom on our television screens, as so many did!

Yootha shot to popularity in the *Fenn Street Gang* and *On The Buses*, but Brian really came to prominence playing the hen-pecked husband George Roper in *Man About The House*. So successful was this first series that the couple eventually got a series of their own using their *Man About the House* character names: *George and Mildred*.

They were seen by the public as a couple, and when I started using them they were the first celebrities for whom I made a joint Greshpic.

I am surprised that they continued working with me after one rather dramatic appearance – or rather our journey to the venue. I will never forget the date: 9 March 1978. They were appearing at a theatre in Birmingham, and I needed to get them to Horsforth in West Yorkshire. I booked them into a hotel in Harrogate, which was only a short drive from the venue. My problem was that I had had an accident and my leg was in plaster, so I had to hire a driver. We both went to collect them, picked them up in Birmingham and headed back north to Harrogate. Brian and Yootha were exhausted after their theatre appearance, so I suggested they get some well-deserved sleep during the journey. Unfortunately I fell asleep as well, and only woke up some hours later. Checking the motorway signs, to my horror I realised we were miles past our turn-off. Our driver didn't have a clue where Harrogate was and was expecting me to give him directions. We were well on our way to Carlisle, and had to turn back. We eventually got to Harrogate at about 5am, which gave Brian and Yootha about three hours' sleep before they were due at the venue. It was an extremely embarrassing moment for The Gresh.

Yootha Joyce.

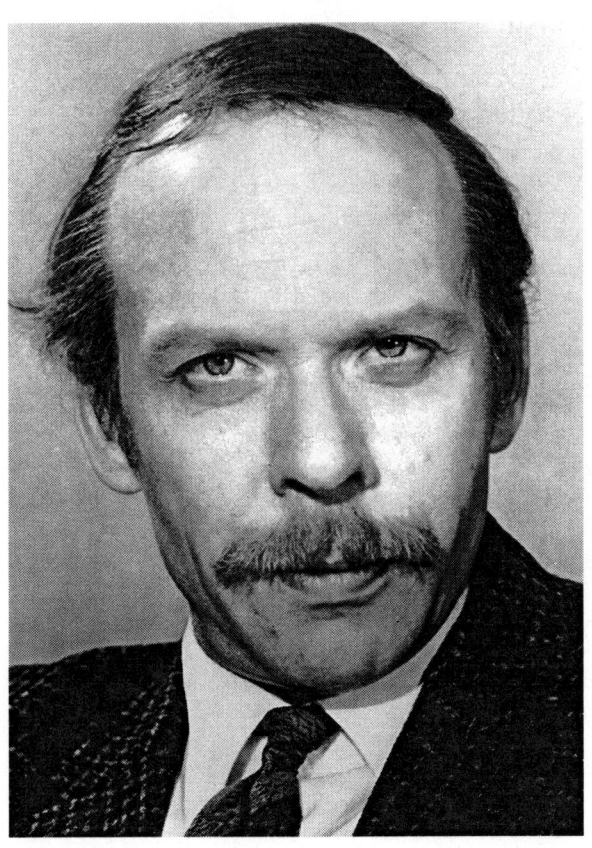

Brian Murphy.

BILL KENWRIGHT's company, Bill Kenwright Ltd, is now the UK's largest independent theatre and film production company.

Bill Kenwright

Bill is another of my celebrities that I still keep in touch with. He has moved on from his role in *Coronation Street* and has become one of our foremost theatre impresarios. Bill did a few PAs for me after we met on the set of *Coronation Street*. I had a small role in a few episodes, and if you look very carefully you can see me in the background in the Rovers Return. Bill was playing Gordon Clegg, and he and Reggie Marsh, who played Dave Smith, the bookie, got together and formed a production company. They staged a few productions such as *Billy Liar*. My involvement was in trying to promote their productions, and it was through this venture that we became friends. Bill later opened an ice rink in Leeds; Yorkshire Television is built on the site now.

On one occasion we were driving back home when Bill said he needed to stop and get something to eat. When we got into the shop Bill noticed a little old lady standing at the counter. She didn't look as if she had a lot of money, simply by the way she was dressed, and Bill felt sorry for her. He emptied all the change he had in his pocket into her hand – a strange gesture, perhaps, but he felt he needed to help her and he was in a position to do so.

Ronald Magill and Arthur Pentelow

When ARTHUR PENTELOW was first acting professionally he made ends meet between engagements by delivering laundry and selling ice creams.

RONALD MAGILL's sideburns were a trademark of his character Amos Brearley – but they weren't planned: he arrived for his audition straight from a play set in Edwardian times, and fully expected to have to shave them off if he bagged the TV role!

Amos Brearley and Mr Wilkes from *Emmerdale Farm* were two other favourites on the PA scene who loved visiting the clubs and galas. As landlord of the Woolpack, Ronald, alias Amos, was once asked to open a new pub in Lancashire. They couldn't pay a fee but were happy to offer him a pint and a sandwich. We declined that offer.

One offer we did accept was from Barratt Homes, who wanted both characters to open a new show house in the North East. We were told to turn up at Leeds Bradford airport, from where we would be flown to the venue in the Barratt helicopter, regularly seen on their TV adverts. I wasn't a fan of flying, and was extremely happy to find out that because of the weather we had to drive up. We arrived two hours late, but both actors did their bit and got stuck in to signing autographs. Ronnie said on the way back that it was the longest two hour appearance he had ever made.

Austin Mitchell and Richard Whiteley

Both were presenters of regional news programme *Calendar* for Yorkshire Television. Austin did a PA for me at The Talk of Yorkshire in Bradford, compèring the Miss Talk of Yorkshire competition in 1974. It wasn't until six years later that I managed to get Richard to do a store opening.

Both were extremely popular presenters, so people wanted to meet them: they were on our screens five nights a week, which was more than some of the actors I was booking. Richard went on to become the presenter of ITV's *Countdown* show until his untimely death in 2005. I had only just managed to get Richard to agree to come on my BCB show and be interviewed a few weeks before he went into hospital. Richard asked me before making the booking what kind of audience figure I got. I told him that if he agreed to come and do the show it would probably double!

AUSTIN MITCHELL became an MP in 1977, and is credited with bringing TV cameras to the House of Commons.

Bob Monkhouse

Bob was a comedy legend, I think you will agree. He built his career on the variety circuit and became one of our best-loved comedians, never short of a gag or story. My first meeting with Bob was before I ran my PA agency, when I was doing some work for the owner of the legendary Batley Variety Club in West Yorkshire. One of my duties was to make sure there was someone to greet the celebrities when they arrived at the club, usually in the afternoon. The billing was always one singer and one comedian, so imagine my horror when I noticed we had ended up with two comedians. On the bill were Bob and a chap called Ray

Fell. Bob handled the situation extremely well and courteously. He normally went on stage at about 11pm, so Ray finished his act, then popped into Bob's dressing room to tell him roughly what gags he'd done so Bob didn't duplicate them. Ray did his fifty minute act, came off stage and told Bob what he'd done. Then Bob went on and did an hour and a half without a single repeated gag, and brought the house down. That in my opinion is comic genius.

Bob's TV credits at the time were for *The Golden Shot* and *Candid Camera*, so there were always plenty of punters wanting to meet him. Unlike many people I have worked with, Bob was always punctual and organised his own travel. This normally unnerved me, but he could always be relied on to be where he was meant to be at the right time. It made my life so much easier.

Morecambe & Wise
Definitely the biggest double act I ever worked with, they could draw a massive crowd and keep them enthralled. I remember talking to their agent Billy Marsh before I first used them. I requested a couple of photographs to use on my Greshpics promotions. Billy asked why I wanted photographs – as surely the public knew what they looked like!

With Eric Morecambe.

 ERIC MORECAMBE took his stage name from Morecambe in Lancashire, where he was born. Since 1999 a larger than lifesize statue of the comic has stood on the promenade there – and it is now one of the most visited attractions in the north-west.

On 1 January 1985 ERNIE WISE made the first mobile phone call in the UK – from St Katherine's Dock in East London to Vodafone's headquarters in Newbury, Berkshire.

It was Ernie who dealt with the business side of their partnership, so it was to him the contracts went. He always wanted to know what the fee was and what expenses they would receive. I got every single receipt from Ernie, accounting for every penny he had spent, but nothing from Eric. He always used to say, 'Don't worry – it'll be fine.'

Eric told me about the car park attendant at the BBC who had his favourites, which meant some would get a parking place and others might not. George was his name. He had lost an arm in the war. One day he shouted to Eric after he had parked the car to ask if there was any chance of tickets for the Christmas show they were going in to record. Eric shouted back, 'No'. George was shocked and asked why. Eric said, 'What's the point? You've only got one arm and you won't be able to clap!' Eric never missed a chance for a gag. If you are wondering, George did get his tickets.

Pete Murray

The DJ and actor Pete Murray was another extremely popular star, particularly with the ladies. He was very popular at the Top Rank bingo halls and we worked together on many occasions. I have already mentioned some bizarre moments in

PETE MURRAY's 1975 autobiography is called *One Day I'll Forget my Trousers*, referring to his days acting in farces in provincial theatres.

my life, and working with Pete brings another one to mind. When we were working together Pete was going out with Valerie Singleton of *Blue Peter* fame. We were sitting in the lounge of Pete's flat in Montague Gardens in London when the phone rang and Pete answered it. All I heard him say was, 'Who's calling?' Obviously someone wanted to speak to Valerie. Peter then followed with 'Anne who?' to which the caller apparently responded, 'The Princess variety!' Yes, it was Princess Anne on the phone for Valerie, hoping to discuss a charity project they were working on together. It's a surreal life sometimes.

Valerie's co-presenter on *Blue Peter*, Peter Purvis, worked with me on a couple of occasions. I remember we went to Holyhead on Anglesey to open a newly refurbished Woolworths store. Peter had a career long before his *Blue Peter* stint, working first in *Z Cars* and then rising to the dizzy heights of the Doctor's travelling companion alongside William Hartnell. This role lasted twenty-eight episodes before he was asked to audition by the BBC for a presenter's role on *Blue Peter*. His new career lasted a little longer, with appearances in over 900 episodes.

JON PERTWEE went to the Royal Academy of Dramatic Arts after he left school – but was expelled for writing rude words on the lavatory wall.

Jon Pertwee

I was able to work with Jon on two levels, as Dr Who and as children's favourite Worzel Gummidge. We attended Dr Who events and conventions to do question and answer sessions and sign autographs, but it was as Worzel Gummidge that he never ceased to amaze me. He never once went out of character all the time he was in front of the public. Even when I interviewed him for the radio he remained the Worzel character.

Pat Phoenix

Who can forget the feisty Elsie Tanner from *Coronation Street*? What a character both on screen and off. I suppose it would be true to say that she always thought she was the star of the show. The producers were always at pains to say that the show didn't have individual stars, but I think the public had their favourites, and it was characters like Pat who had the juicy story lines.

As with *Emmerdale Farm*, the public wanted to see all their favourites, so I was always being asked to book as many actors as possible.

I have already mentioned the rivalry between Pat and some of the other cast members. As always, it came down to money.

Pat always insisted that she was known by her real name; just like Frazer Hines, she hated people calling her by her character name. She didn't mind so much from children, but got quite irate if an adult referred to her as Elsie Tanner.

A personal appearance by Pat Phoenix.

Through her last marriage, to Tony Booth, PAT PHOENIX became the stepmother of Cherie Blair and mother-in-law of Tony Blair.

Pat employed a manager and driver called Bill Nadin, who went everywhere with her; even on the PAs we did. He lived with her, generally took care of her and was one of the few people who could tolerate her moods and outbursts. I often heard him being criticised, which was a shame because he was a nice man.

I remember going to see a play that Pat was in. I was sitting with another of the *Street*'s stars, Betty Driver, who played Betty Turpin (who worked behind the bar at the Rovers Return). The play was quite heavy, I suppose you could say, and Pat was deep into her part arguing with a fellow character. When they finished the applause was a little while in coming, and then Betty and I overheard an elderly lady behind us say, 'That sorted her out, Elsie.' So many people could only view Pat as Elsie Tanner. I suppose in a way that's stardom.

After the play ended Betty and I went backstage to see Pat, and she asked us what we thought of her performance. To Betty's credit she said, 'I've never seen you work harder,' neither saying whether she liked it or hated it – true diplomacy from a fellow actor.

John Russell, 13th Duke of Bedford

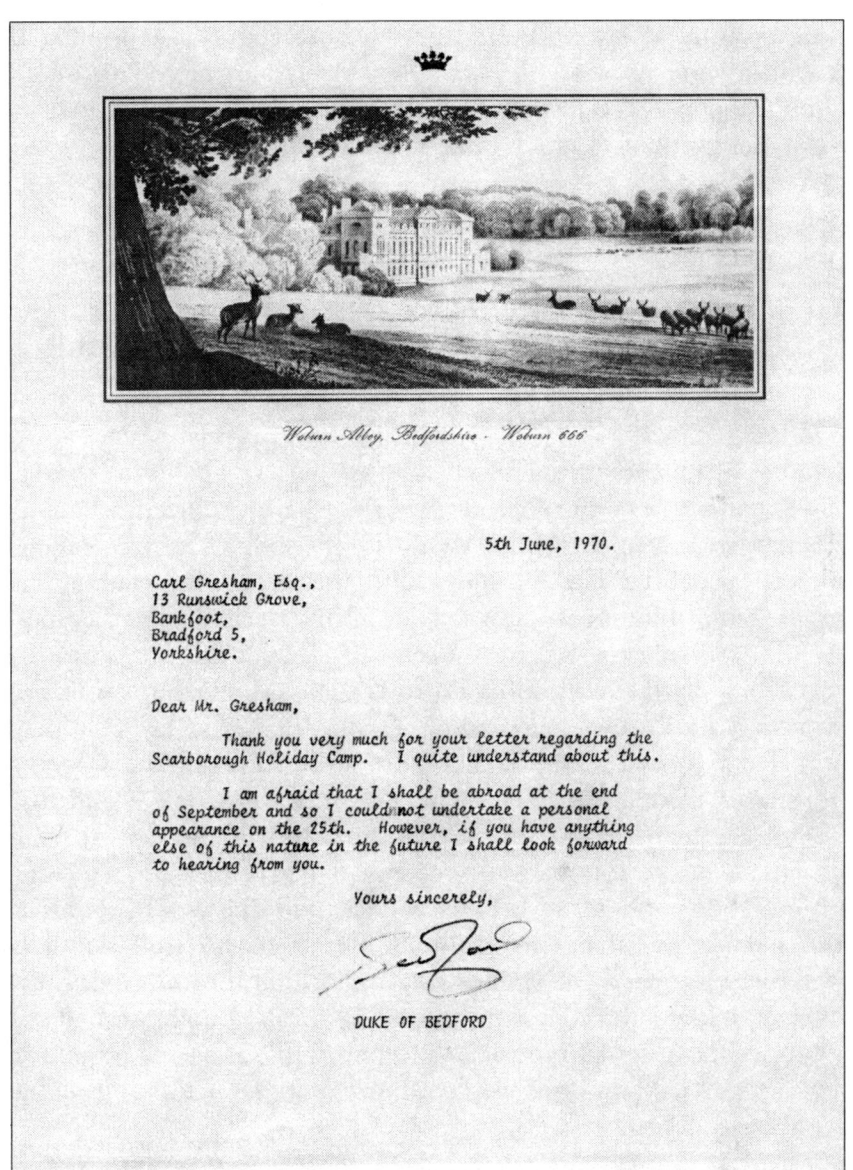

Probably the most unusual 'celebrity' I ever employed was, to give him his full name and title, His Grace the Duke of Bedford, John Robert Russell, 13th Duke of Bedford, owner of Woburn Abbey, which is today best known as a safari park. As with many of our aristocracy he faced massive death duties, nearly £4m, at the time of his father's death and needed to look at how the estate and the family could be maintained. The Duke came to the attention of Dudley Wallis of holiday camp fame, who wanted to meet him – why I am not sure. I thought I would give it a go and see if the idea appealed to the Duke, so I rang Woburn Abbey and made enquiries. A few days afterwards my secretary passed a call to me, and when I answered all I heard was, 'Bedford here'. It took me a while to work out who it was. We discussed the proposal that he would make a few appearances, firstly at the request of Dudley Wallis and then anything else I could come up with. We were both a little unsure about how popular he would prove: would anyone want to meet a duke? As it transpired, no they didn't. I booked him to open a Woolworth branch shortly afterwards, but that was it. My short involvement with aristocracy came to an abrupt end.

The 13th DUKE OF BEDFORD's first job was as a rent collector in Stepney – before joining the Coldstream Guards.

David Whitfield

David was one of this country's finest 'lounge singers', and I am proud to say I was his personal manager throughout the '70s. David enjoyed a lengthy career, hitting the number one spot in June 1954 with his song *Cara Mia,* which went on to be an international hit. There is little doubt that his charm, charisma and vocal dexterity won him thousands of new fans in his later years, and we always carried a quantity of glossy photographs for David to sign for his admirers. In 1974 I pushed extremely hard for Phonogram to record a new album with him, and I can tell you they took much persuading. Finally, in 1975, the Chappell Studios were booked and David went in to record with some of the country's finest session musicians. Along with Len Hunter as musical arranger and director we had a marvellous team to record this album – but it did not go well. David struggled with his voice for many hours until I had a thought. He was used to working late nights in clubs and cabaret venues, and that was when his voice was at its best. I suggested that David should return to his hotel until later that evening, and we organised the orchestra to record all the music during the day. David returned in the late evening to record his vocals. Bingo: we had ourselves a record. Many of those session musicians followed this David Whitfield recording with a new album for Mantovani, while others went off to Abbey Road to record a new Geoff Love album.

DAVID WHITFIELD's hit 'Cara Mia' spent ten weeks at Number One. Today, more than fifty years on, he is one of only six artists to have achieved this.

It was many years later that I had a call from a gentleman by the name of Ivan Trusler, who asked if I had been David Whitfield's manager. I was intrigued and said I had. Ivan explained that he had the rights to the album, *Hey there it's David Whitfield,* and would like to re-issue it on CD. Would I be involved? I was delighted that someone had seen fit to get David's music back in the public domain at last. Ivan and the team at Brevan Records did a brilliant job in producing the CD, and I cannot thank them enough. They have managed to include two live tracks as well. If you would like to get a copy you can get it from their website: www.brevanrecords.co.uk.

I still play David Whitfield's music on my BCB radio show, much to the delight of many listeners. Sadly he died in Australia in 1980.

Mike and Bernie Winters
I will be eternally grateful to Mike and Bernie Winters for one episode that occurred when I had booked them to do a PA. They had been booked to do a week's cabaret at a club in Chesterfield. After the booking had been made and they had agreed to come up I found out that the club was having financial difficulties, and there was a likelihood of them not getting paid. I had committed to publicity for the PA and was extremely worried that they wouldn't want to do it if the club date had been cancelled; after all, they would be travelling up from London so they wouldn't just come to do my event. As Mike said at the time, it was a good thing that they travelled together in one Rolls!

Sadly Bernie is no longer with us, but I was able to have Mike on my BCB radio show last year.

Crowds gather to see Peter Wyngarde.

Peter Wyngarde

Suave, sophisticated, French-born and a winner with the ladies. Peter Wyngarde made his name playing Jason King in *Department S,* later getting his own series. He played roles in many of the early '70s TV dramas such as *The Baron, The Prisoner, The Saint* and *The Avengers.*

Peter drew some of the biggest crowds we ever had – mainly ladies who absolutely adored him, much to the disappointment and irritation of their menfolk, it must be said. His exotic looks and background were backed up by a voice that was once described as 'black magic'.

Peter was a firm favourite with Woolworths for their store openings. They knew that the crowds and the publicity would be huge. On one occasion Peter and I were stopped by police officers on the outskirts of Barnsley and asked not to proceed, as they were worried about being able to control the crowd outside the Woolworth store we were going to. This created a fantastic story for the national press, which featured one headline declaring 'Jason King barred from town centre'.

PETER WYNGARDE's only LP, entitled *When Sex Leers Its Inquisitive Head,* was issued in 1970 and withdrawn weeks later. It is described by the record company that recently issued it on CD as 'one of pop's more bizarre offerings' . . .

Bernard Youens

Bernard was another of my *Coronation Street* favourites. He played Stan Ogden opposite Jean Alexander's character, his wife Hilda; it was another of those unforgettable TV partnerships. Bernard and I worked so closely together that he eventually asked me to become his manager, which I was more than happy to do. Bernard was a true gentleman, a total contrast to the working-class, vest-wearing slob that he portrayed in the programme.

We were travelling back from a PA one afternoon. As we drove through Richmond in North Yorkshire Bernard declared that he needed a drink. I pointed out that it was ten to four and pubs would be shut. He told me to find a pub that did bed and breakfast, which I finally did. We went in, and of course he was instantly recognised. 'How are you, Stan?' said the owner. In contrast to Pat Phoenix or Frazer Hines, Bernard wasn't bothered about being referred to by his character's name.

We went up to the bar and Bernard asked if there was any chance we might have a drink. The owner said unfortunately not, as we weren't residents. Bernard asked how much rooms were and was told £15, which was a lot of money back then. He immediately booked one, then asked if, as he was now a resident, he

A newspaper dubbed BERNARD YOUENS's character, Stan Ogden, as 'the uncrowned king of the non-working classes'.

could have a drink. The owner was happy to oblige. Bernard ordered a pint, and I had a soft drink as I was driving. We drank up, then Bernard handed the room keys back to the owner, said thank you, and we left. To say the owner was stunned would be an understatement. Bernard had been happy to pay for a room simply so he could have a drink.

Jimmy Young

Jimmy was always a pleasure to work with and a favourite with the Top Rank bingo organisation. On one of our events I arrived at my hotel to find a message from him saying that he wouldn't be appearing at the Hackney Top Rank Club as arranged, because he never appeared with another celebrity and had met a fan who had told him she was looking forward to meeting the star hairdresser Raymonde at the event. I was horrified, because I knew Sir Jimmy liked to be the only celebrity, and wondered if Top Rank had booked someone else without telling me. I rang their head office immediately and they told me to look at the ad placed in the evening paper. The advert stated that Jimmy Young would have Raymondo with him.

Those of you who remember Jimmy's radio show may remember that he used to have a 'recipe of the day' spot; he would say, 'What's the recipe for today, Raymondo?' The lady who had taken the details for the ad had mistakenly thought it was something to do with the famous hairdresser of the time who was also called Raymondo.

Radio Days

Having worked at a number of radio stations I have been privileged to meet many personalities over the years.

One that springs to mind from my Radio Aire days is Sir David Frost. I tried to interview him as he was about to step into a taxi to take him to the station, and although he hadn't time to stop he said I could join him on the journey. What an opportunity, I thought, and hopped in. Imagine my horror when I returned to the studio to find I hadn't pressed the record button.

I interviewed stage actor Ron Moody when I was at Pennine, having been called to say he was in reception and wasn't best pleased about being kept waiting. When I got to see him he said he would give me five minutes. I first asked him how different Fagin was in the stage version from the film version. Over an hour later we were still talking!

Another of my favourite radio interviews was with the *Good Old Days* producer Barney Colehan. You may remember that the show was broadcast from the Leeds City Varieties – not the most modern of theatres but with a long history and tradition of variety shows. Singing star Eartha Kitt had been booked to appear, and when she arrived she was disappointed at the poor standard of her dressing room. In truth the whole theatre was pretty poor as it was so old. She made a complaint to Barney, who told her that she had been allocated the dressing room once used by Charlie Chaplin. Not another word was heard: she was extremely happy to be in the same room as the great man had been.

Many years later she returned to the theatre and asked if she could have Charlie Chaplin's old dressing room again. She was allocated to a different one, and went straight to Barney to ask why. Quick as a flash he said, 'He visited more than once, you know.'

Some years later I asked Barney how he knew which dressing rooms Charlie Chaplin had used; he said he had no idea which they were!

The Bachelors.

I still do my Sunday morning show on BCB, the Bradford Community Radio station, which has enabled me to have a constant stream of guests to interview and chat to. Over the last few years I have had the privilege of interviewing magician Paul Daniels and his wife Debbie McGee, comedian Jimmy Cricket, soul legend Tommy Hunt, Con Clusky of The Bachelors, Mike Pender from The Searchers, Mike Winters of Mike and Bernie Winters fame, actors Roy Hudd and Ricky Tomlinson, and friend and international concert pianist John Briggs is always a welcome guest on my show.

Some of the others that I have been lucky enough to have worked with or who have visited the studio and my show, and haven't been mentioned anywhere above, are Ken Kitson, Duncan Norvelle, Mark Wynter, Paul Jones, P.J. Proby, Jess Conrad, Edward Woodward, Frank Carson, Derek Batey, Cannon and Ball, The Krankies, Dickie Henderson, Brenda Lee, Russell Harty, Tommy Trinder and, to finish up with a group, the Kings Singers.

With Bill Wyman.

With Kiki Dee.

It is always a pleasure to have my friend and local author Derek A.J. Lister on the show. We have had many happy hours talking about the city in which we both live and the music we have enjoyed in the past. Derek has always been jealous of me getting to meet and have my photograph taken with Jayne Mansfield, but I have always been jealous of Derek's meeting with Laurel and Hardy, which I think beats me hands down.

One of the highlights of my time at BCB had to be when Bill Wyman, ex-bassist of the Rolling Stones, came to the studio. Bill was on a publicity tour promoting his book *The Rolling Stones: A History in Cartoons*. We were able to chat for over an hour and it's a show I will never forget. It was quite a coup for the radio station to have someone of Bill's reputation on air, and a great thrill for me to be able to interview him.

While I never worked with her I want to give Kiki Dee a mention. Kiki is a Bradford girl and I have had the pleasure of her company on many occasions. I will never forget her performance at Bradford's St George's Hall. Kiki's duet with Elton John, *Don't Go Breaking My Heart*, gave Elton his first UK number one. As she started to perform the song there was one obvious problem: no Elton. Well, there wouldn't be in Bradford, would there? But just as the opening riff started up we were amazed to see Elton John walk on to the stage so he and Kiki could perform their number one hit together. Helen and I were invited backstage by Kiki and got to meet Elton. As we walked into the dressing room Kiki introduced Elton and he said, 'Hello, I'm Elton John,' to which Helen answered, 'I know you're Elton John, I'm Helen Gresham.' During the conversation we learnt that he had chartered a plane, costing him £5,000 an hour, so he could get back to London the same night. It was quite a surreal experience, totally unexpected and one we'll both never forget.

With Paul Daniels.

Superslam Wrestling and the Foam Hands

You may ask what The Gresh does these days. Well, the celebrity appearance scene has long since vanished, but I do have another rather unusual business which has proved very successful over the years. When I was managing Stuart Damon, Craig Stirling in *The Champions,* he embarked on a singing career alongside his acting, and for reasons I never fathomed he was invited to represent Britain in a singing contest in Bogotá, Colombia. As he was an American this came as a surprise, as did the unexpected country that was hosting the event. We duly set off and flew from Heathrow to Antigua, then on to Colombia. I think he was thirty-fourth out of forty, so it wasn't the most successful venture.

Stuart suggested that on the way home we could fly back via New York so he could visit his parents. We arrived and booked into a hotel, and Stuart set off to visit family and friends. I was mesmerised by American TV, so many channels and such variety, so I started channel hopping, and eventually came across an American football game. I have no interest in sport whatsoever and was just about to switch off when I noticed the cheerleaders. Besides being rather gorgeous, they were all waving what looked like huge foam hands. Then I noticed that the crowd had them too. This gave me an idea, and as soon as I arrived home I looked around for a manufacturer of foam products in the UK.

My idea was to offer the same idea to British promoters of sports and theatre productions. I rang round a few companies and was told that manufacturing something like this would be very expensive as they had to make moulds, but I managed to get one company to give it a go. I drew up an outline of what I wanted and added the word 'Boo'. My intention was to offer the product to pantomime producers for audience participation. Not only could the audience shout, they could wave these outsize foam hands!

To say the hands took off is an understatement, and for many years I have supplied a variety of theatres with these foam products. I soon realised that any logo or wording could be printed on them, and I started looking around for other opportunities. This led me to a relationship which is still running to this day.

Superslam Wrestling Promotions™ is run by my dear friend Brian Dixon. Brian has run these wrestling events around the country for many years, and now features wrestlers with some wonderful and colourful names, such as Gladiator Oblivion, Highlander, Gangrel, El Ligero. There are also women such as Miss Britani, Lisa Fury and a female tag duo called Team Blossom: they sound so sweet, don't they? Brian takes his shows all round the country and has exclusive rights to shows at Butlins in Skegness, Bognor Regis and Minehead. As long as Brian is running his shows I'll be happy to supply him with this unique product.

Derek Franks

I would like to conclude my story with a tribute to my dear friend and colleague Derek Franks, who sadly died last year. I received a phone call from our mutual friend Frazer Hines to say that Derek's wife Debra had given him the news. I was in shock. Derek and I had worked together when I formed Greshstyle Personal Appearances; he had been my compère and 'booker' at events. Derek had been around the club scene as half of a singing duo and was keen to move into management himself, so I knew he would eventually leave and set up his own business.

I remember Derek ringing me to say he had booked his first star. It was the singer Gerry Marsden: that was the beginning of their thirty year personal and professional relationship.

Debra has carried on with the agency, and along with their daughters Nikki and Kirsty arranged a show at the Batley Frontier Club in May this year to celebrate Derek's life, which I was delighted and proud to attend. Stars who appeared were many and varied: The Manfreds, featuring Paul Jones, Brian Poole from The Tremeloes, Chris Farlowe, Vanity Fare, P.J. Proby, Dave Berry, Maggie Bell, Mike Pender of The Searchers and TV's *X Factor* contestants Journey South, along with the wonderful Martin Gold as compère for the evening. There were special guest appearances by Frazer Hines, Bev Bevan of ELO fame and magician and illusionist Shahid Malik. It was a very special night and a fitting tribute to a man we all loved, and had the added bonus of raising over £15,000 for a Variety Club of Great Britain Sunshine coach, which will carry Derek's name. Donations were also made to some local charities.

Frazer and I loved being in the company of Derek and Debra, and have many happy memories of those occasions.

Sadly I never managed to get Derek in to record one of my shows, despite him being keen and asking when he could do it. I always thought it was an imposition to get him over early on a Sunday morning from his house in Kexby near York to record it, but Debra was kind enough to come over and do a live show with Frazer Hines and Martin Gold to promote the charity show and to fulfil that promise.

Rest in peace, my dear friend.

Derek and Debra Franks at Gretna Green.

Finale

Well that's it: my story is up to date. I am still doing my radio show each Sunday. It has been an exciting life so far, and very enjoyable. I have been privileged to work with many of the stars of stage, screen and TV, and many of them still visit me to appear on my weekly radio show.

April 2009 saw another of my birthday parties in Bradford. I was hoping one of my friends, actor Ken Kitson, who you may know best as the policeman in *Last of the Summer Wine*, would be able to attend, but unfortunately filming commitments wouldn't allow. However, he did send me this wonderful poem, which I would like to use in conclusion to my story.

The Gresh: a birthday tribute April 2009
by Ken Kitson: actor.

No cards or pressies were requested
Hee hee, just think of the cake candles invested.
You who have met the world's famous faces
One to one, no heirs and graces.
Jayne Mansfield, Bill Wyman, Eric and Ernie, Kiki Dee
Gordon Jackson, Larry Grayson and my fave Brenda Lee.
Martin Shaw, Hughie Green and many many more,
The list is endless, impossible to keep the score.
Starting your days as a cheeky local DJ,
enjoying the work, new ventures each day.
The stories you tell some think are fable,
but true through many nights at the round table.
Your work and research exudes from the wireless, the chats,
enjoyment and energy forever tireless.

With joy of meeting people not to be faulted
making each guest feel special, years never halted.
Your record collection speaks for itself
with strong support under every shelf.
Still going strong with interest and fun,
the love of the job, same as when you begun.
Great luck with your book, good future behold,
hoping for lots of sales when your life's pages unfold.
So keep your airtime interesting,
amusing and fresh,
from me and all your friends,
Happy birthday to The Gresh!

What does the future hold for The Gresh?

A TV series based on the book would be rather lovely, along with a theatre tour to talk and reminisce about those days. Possibly pantomime, but I'm too old for Buttons . . . 'Oh yes I am . . .'

A portrait of The Gresh by Lesley Piper.

With actor and poet Ken Kitson.

With Garth Cawood.

With Derek A J Lister at Morrison's Bradford signing copies of *Bradford's Own* in front of the *Calendar* local evening news crew.

Best of British Comedy gathering at St George's Hall, Bradford.

Cover of the *Bradford Pictorial*, signed by the Beatles.

ALEXANDRA BASTEDO

She's a super girl! And the word "super" describes not only the character Alexandra Bastedo plays in *The Champions* — Sharron Macready, and as Diana Dalzell in *Codename*, but the strikingly beautiful young blonde herself.

Stardom came to her at the age of twenty-one (she was born on 9th March, 1946). A friend suggested that Alex should enter the contest to find a "Teen-age Diplomat," the winner to go to Hollywood to appear in *The Candy Webb* (retitled *13 Frightened Girls* in England). She did — one of 4,000 girls to do so. And she won.

So at the age of 16, she went to Hollywood to make her screen debut. And this proved to be the somewhat devious trail to her winning the feminine lead in *The Champions*.

She is a girl who loves travelling and her many visits to the continent have provided her with a fluent knowledge of French and Italian.

RAY BARRETT (Peter Thornton of *The Troubleshooters*)

Born in Australia. Started work at the age of eleven in a radio play for the Australian Broadcasting Commission. Joined a local radio station as a disc jockey and continued to work in radio and in the theatre in Australia, both acting and singing.

He came to the U.K. in 1959 and appeared for ten months in *Emergency-Ward 10*. His films include *Mix Me A Person*, *Jigsaw* and *Reptiles*. In 1965 he created the part of 'Peter Thornton' in the highly successful B.B.C. T.V. series *The Troubleshooters* and he has just completed work on the sixth series of this programme.

Recently re-commenced his career as a singer and his L.P. record *No Trouble Now* was released last year, together with a single, *If You Go Away*, and a new album is in preparation. His principal hobby is golf (handicap 9) and he has just completed the building of his house on the island of Formentera, off Ibiza.

Guess who's coming to Wallis's this week?
By arrangement with CARL GRESHAM PROMOTIONS

LIZ GEBHARDT
(Maureen of *Please Sir*)

Liz Gebhardt was born in Liverpool — her mother is Welsh and her father American — but she has spent most of her life in London. She trained for the theatre at Guildhall School of Music and Drama, and began her career at the Castle Theatre, Farnham, where she played a wide variety of parts from Ophelia in *Hamlet* to Nancy in *The Knack*. Her theatre work also includes seasons at the Liverpool Playhouse, the Phoenix, Leicester, etc. She made guest appearances as Alice in *Alice Through The Looking Glass* and Jane in *Jane Eyre*. She has played in many television productions including Maureen Bullock in the series *Please Sir* and leading roles in episodes from popular series as *Blackmail*, *Z Cars*, *Half Hour Story*, etc.

Miss SHEILA SCOTT, O.B.E.

Started flying in 1959 in England. Her first aircraft was a biplane, a Tiger Moth - Jackaroo, known as 'Myth' (a female mothl) which she toured and raced all over Europe. Now flies all types of light aircraft. Is primarily a competitive, racing and ferry pilot. Competes in most major international competitive events, as well as record attempts.

She now holds 91 World 'Class' Records. Her first records were in 1965, when in two days she broke 15 World 'Class' inter-capital records in a Piper Comanche 400('Myth Sunpip'). These were followed by the 'Round the World Records' in Class C.I.c. and the Open Feminine Class May/June, 1966 in her own Piper Comanche 260 ('Myth Too'). She was also the first British pilot (man or woman) to fly solo round the world and made the longest consecutive solo flight in history of over 31,000 miles in her single engined Comanche. In 1967 in the same aircraft, 'Myth Too,' she broke London to Capetown and Capetown to London records. She also broke North Atlantic East to West direct crossing record to Canada, followed by goodwill tour through U.S.A. to South America where she broke the South Atlantic record, West to East. In May, 1969 she broke her own North Atlantic records during the Transatlantic Air Race in which she won the Women's light aircraft prize as well as new records from London to New York. On the way back she took seven records between New York and Copenhagen. October, 1969, she took further London to Kenya and South Africa, and South Africa to London World Records.

HIS GRACE THE DUKE OF BEDFORD (John Robert Russell)
(*The Thirteenth Duke of Bedford*)

The Thirteenth Duke of Bedford, John Robert Russell was born in 1917. When war broke out he joined the Coldstream Guards but was invalided out after a relatively short time. He became a journalist for the *Sunday Express* and after the death of his wife in 1945 he married again in 1947. When he succeeded to the title he faced a bill for death duties amounting to more than 4 million pounds. The Duke fought hard to eventually retain Woburn Abbey both as an heirloom and as his home. Under the Duke's personal direction Woburn has continued to develop and expand its activities since it was opened to the public in 1955, and with his present wife Nicole, whom he married in 1960, they work incessantly on new ideas that will interest visitors.

REGINALD MARSH
(Dave Smith of *Coronation Street*)
Reginald Marsh has been popping in and out of *Coronation Street* for over five years, between times he has made many dramatic roles become the highlight of a series, such as his part of works manager in *The Planemakers*. He began acting in 1942 and among his T.V. credits are featured roles in *Shadow Squad* and *The Champions*. His films have included *The Day the Earth Caught Fire* and *Jigsaw*. In private life Reginald is married to actress Rosemary Murray and they have three children, Adam, Rebecca and Alison. Apart from collecting antiques, Reginald spends his spare time writing plays and at the moment he is working on a comedy.

PENNY SPENCER
(Sharron of *Please Sir*)
Penny Spencer was born in Hillingdon, Middlesex and moved to Kingston on Thames, Surrey when she was one year old. A chance meeting in a Wimpy Bar with the Principal of Cambridge Manor School began her way into the acting profession. Though she can't remember her very first television appearance she was kept busy during her training days at Drama School. She loves working and has many credits for T.V. appearances which include *Paul Temple, Call My Bluff, Frost on Sunday, Mr. Rose, Dixon of Dock Green* and of course her part as Sharon Everleigh in the award winning London Weekend Television series of *Please Sir* which is starting a new series later this year. Penny likes to play a variety of parts and have peace of mind. Her cinema appearances have included *Sleep is Lovely, The Best House in London, Isadora* and *The Whisperers* in which she played Avis Bunnage's daughter.

DAVID HAMILTON
David started in T.V. as a continuity script writer at the tender age of 17. He worked for a time as an Announcer and D.J. for B.F.N. in Germany before becoming a T.V. Announcer in 1961. He has appeared for every I.T.V. Company in Britain and for six years he was A.B.C.'s star announcer in the North. Tyne Tees viewers voted him Personality of the Year and a Daily Express poll placed him in the top ten T.V. personalities in Britain. Ken Dodd christened him "Diddy David" and gained him a whole new army of fans. On radio he has compered more than 500 shows including *Family Choice; Mid-day Spin*, and his own *David Hamilton Show*. David enjoys football and has recently acquired a race horse called "Try for Ten" after his successful Anglia T.V. series.

The management regrets that due to the time factor and large number of people, it will not be possible for our guests from the 'World of Television' to sign autographs individually.

However, 1,000 autographed photo-prints will be available at a minimum price of 6d. each. The proceeds will go to the Holidays for Handicapped Children Fund (see *page 31*).

WILLIAM GAUNT
(Richard Barrett of *The Champions*)
Bill Gaunt was born in Pudsey, Yorkshire, the son of a lawyer. In his final year in R.A.D.A. he auditioned, successfully, for the Garfield Weston Fellowship Training Course at Wace University, Dallas, Texas, the late Charles Laughton being one of the judges.
For the next year he alternated between the theatre, T.V. and films until he was offered the part of Bob Marriott in the *Sergeant Cork* series which occupied him for the next three years. Throughout 1967 he played the part of Richard Barrett in the filmed T.V. series of *The Champions*. 1968 brought him the opportunity to play opposite Barbara Murray in *The Flip Side* at the Appollo Theatre, London and following this he played Lawrence in the B.B.C.2 series *Tenant of Wildfell Hall*, after which he again appeared in the West End with the part of Hank in *The Boys in the Band* at Wyndhams.

GORDEN KAYE
(Bernard — Elsie Tanner's nephew in *Coronation Street*)
Knock on Elsie Tanner's door and you will probably come face-to-face with disaster on two legs. The legs belong not to Elsie but to her gangling, accident-prone nephew Bernard Butler, played by 28-year-old Gorden Kaye. Gorden was born in Huddersfield and christened Gorden with an 'O'. 'The spelling,' says Gorden, 'got changed by coincidence.'
'I wrote off for an application form to join Equity, and it came back addressed to Gorden Kaye, and, before I had time to fill it in, I got whisked into hospital — where I found the name on the chart at the top of my bed was also spelled Gorden.' 'I decided it was just too much of a coincidence to ignore, so I went along with it and have been Gorden ever since.'
He joined Bradford Playhouse, commuting every night from Huddersfield. 'It's a 27-mile journey,' he says, 'and I reckon I must have clocked up 14,000 miles during the four years I was with the Playhouse company.'
Gorden was offered a small part in a radio play at Leeds, and that led to his first T.V. part in *Champion House* and then to parts in Roy Kinnear's series and in *The Flaxton Boys*.

GRAHAM HABERFIELD
(Winston of *The Dustbinmen*)
Born 1941. Married with two children (boys). Two years training at Bristol Old Vic Theatre School.
Joined *Coronation Street* 1962 — left to appear in West End run and other television work which included a *No Hiding Place* series — rejoined the *Street* and last August took an 'acting holiday' to star in *Rattle of a Simple Man* at Bradford Alhambra Theatre. Hobbies include — Shooting, skin diving, driving fast cars, fishing and playing Rugby Union. He says he feels he doesn't have time for anything else.

Continued on next page

23

BUY THESE OTHER BANK HOUSE BOOKS

BRADFORD BORN & BRED
Derek A.J. Lister

A must for anyone with Bradford connections, but everyone who grew up in Britain soon after the war will recognise so much in this big memory filled book.

BRADFORD'S NOISE OF THE VALLEY
Gary Cavanagh
with Matt Webster

An epic first instalment in the rich pageant of Bradford's musical past – photos, family trees, news reports – one of the most comprehensive musical encyclopaedias ever written. If it's not in here, it probably never happened.

MOODS, MOMENTS & MEMORIES
Ken Kitson

Everyone recognises Ken Kitson the actor, with a string of character roles to his credit before his current high profile part in *The Last of the Summer Wine*. Here he reveals his other side, as a thoughtful and perceptive poet, his wide-ranging works enhanced by specially created illustrations from some of Ken's fellow artists.

EYE TO EYE
Cyril Frankel
with a foreword by Alexandra Bastedo

Legendary film, TV and theatre director Cyril Frankel finally lets the world in on his extraordinary life story, from making the first ever film with an all-black non-professional cast (*Man of Africa*) to developing and directing mammothly successful TV series such as *Gideon's Way, The Champions, Department S and Randall & Hopkirk (Deceased)*. As we soon learn from this book, there was a lot more to it than even that.

For more details and ordering, go to
www.bankhousebooks.com